AM I A NARCISSISTIC MOTHER?

Understanding, Healing, and Nurturing Healthy Relationships

DR. SARAH MITCHELL

Copyright©2023 Dr. Sarah Mitchell.

All Rights Reserved. No part of this publication may be reproduced or transmitted, in any form or by any means without permission.

CONTENTS

CHAPTER 1 1

   Self-Evaluation Starts 1

CHAPTER 2 13

   The Narcissistic Temperament 13

CHAPTER 3 29

   Understanding the symptoms 29

CHAPTER 4 43

   The Effects on Your Children 43

CHAPTER 5 57

   Navigating the Blame Game 57

CHAPTER 6 75

   Recovering and Transforming 75

CHAPTER 7 113

   Creating wholesome relationships 113

x

CHAPTER 1

Self-Evaluation Starts

Introduction: The Self-Exploration Journey

Few excursions in the complex tapestry of human existence are as meaningful and transforming as the journey within. The act of introspection, self-awareness, and self-discovery involved in this journey is known as self-exploration. It is a crucial first step in comprehending the intricacies of being a mother with narcissistic tendencies because it serves as the compass that leads us through the maze of our ideas, feelings, and experiences.

Self-exploration has become more important than just therapy in today's environment because it is essential to both personal development and emotional health. Self-examination assumes a special and compelling meaning in the context of motherhood, particularly when addressing the question, "Am I a Narcissistic Mother?"

As the beginning of your transformative journey, this invites you to go out on a path of self-discovery that will help you understand the complex layers of your identity and parenting philosophy. It is the beginning of a journey that will ultimately result in healing, progress, and the development of better connections with your children as you unravel the mysteries of narcissism within yourself.

Effectiveness of Self-Awareness

The powerful force of self-awareness is at the center of self-exploration. It is the lantern that reveals both our strengths and our weaknesses by illuminating the deepest recesses of our soul. The basis for developing our ability for understanding, compassion, and transformation is self-awareness. You are committing to shining the light within by starting this path of self-discovery.

In the end, self-discovery is the key that opens the door to recovery and the development of wholesome relationships. It is a difficult journey, but the rewards are tremendous. It requires courage, honesty, and self-compassion. Keep in mind that as you go out on this journey into the depths of your own psyche, it is a path paved with the possibility of profound transformation as well as self-discovery and progress. It is the first step to developing into the best mother and person you can be.

Accepting Transformation and Realizing the Need for Change

A single, profound realization—the necessity for change—often marks the start of the self-discovery process. We recognize that something is wrong with us at this very moment of awakening and that the status quo is no longer adequate. This realization is a crucial turning point in the process of self-discovery within the context of motherhood and narcissism, one that contains the potential for transformation.

Inconvenient Self-Reflection Mirror

In essence, self-reflection is holding up a mirror to our own spirits. We confront our actions, beliefs, and the effects they have on people around us, especially our children, on this introspective trip. It's a process that calls for bravery because it frequently entails admitting our shortcomings and weaknesses.

This realization can be both unsettling and empowering for a mother who is questioning, "Am I a Narcissistic Mother?" It is uncomfortable because it requires facing actions and routines that may have been harmful, but it is liberating because it creates room for improvement and recovery. Realizing that mothers are not fixed beings but rather have the ability to develop and evolve.

The Change Catalysts

Recognizing the need for change is frequently sparked by different events in our lives. A specific occurrence, a meaningful chat with a loved one, or just a growing sense of discontent with our own behavior may serve as the catalyst for this epiphany. Whatever the cause, it serves as a wake-up call that encourages us to leave our comfort zones and start on a transformational road.

Recognizing the need for change in the context of maternal narcissism can take several forms:

1. Children's Experience: Perhaps it's seeing the emotional toll our actions have on our kids, the sadness in their eyes, or the growing gulf between us. This may serve as a potent catalyst for transformation.

2. Self-Reflection: Self-reflection, as uncomfortable as it may be, can uncover behavioral habits that are no longer consistent with our beliefs or the type of parent we want to be.

3. External input can occasionally serve as a strong reminder that we need to make changes. These observations and comments may come from friends, family members, or experts.

The Way Ahead

While acknowledging the need for change is the first step, it is only the start of a meaningful journey. It is a recognition that we have the ability to change the way our stories are told, to break free from negative habits, and to foster better relationships with our kids.

Remember that accepting the need for change is a sign of strength and perseverance rather than weakness. It is an invitation to embrace change and set out on a path of healing and self-discovery, not only for your own sake but also for the wellbeing of your kids and your family as a whole.

Illuminating the Path to Personal Growth with the Power of Self-Awareness

Self-awareness serves as a guiding light for us as we navigate the winding paths of our inner world during this arduous journey of self-discovery. This beacon carries tremendous potential for change and personal development, in addition to illuminating the contours of our ideas, emotions, and behaviors. The importance of self-awareness cannot be stressed in the context of the book "Am I a Narcissistic Mother? Understanding, Healing, and Nurturing Healthy Relationships." It serves as the cornerstone upon which the structure of change and recovery is constructed.

How to define self-awareness

The ability to consciously identify and comprehend one's own thoughts, emotions, and behaviors is known as self-awareness. It is the capacity to objectively watch oneself, to take a step back from the chaos of daily life, and to gain understanding of one's motivations, values, and objectives. To hold up a mirror to the soul and see both the light and the shadows within is analogous to that.

Self-Awareness and Maternal Narcissism: A Nexus

Self-awareness is the fulcrum on which the transformational journey pivots for a mother who is asking herself, "Am I a Narcissistic Mother?" It is the awareness that one's parenting style may display narcissistic traits; this awareness frequently arises through introspection and open self-evaluation.

The dynamics of a family can be significantly impacted by maternal narcissism, which is characterized by a focus on one's own needs and wants at the expense of a child's mental wellbeing. It could show up in actions like emotional control, a lack of empathy, or a need for constant approval. Without self-awareness, these tendencies may go unchecked and result in harm perpetuation.

The Enlightening Results of Self-Awareness

Self-awareness shines a light into our psyche's shadowy areas. It enables us to

1. Recognize Destructive Patterns: Self-awareness allows us to recognize destructive patterns of action and thought. Often, the first step towards transformation is this recognition.

2. Recognize Triggers: Self-awareness aids in identifying the factors that set off our narcissistic inclinations. Is it fear, trepidation, or previous trauma? Being aware of the underlying reasons helps us find solutions.

3. Develop Empathy: Self-awareness encourages empathy by allowing us to perceive the world from our children's perspectives. It enables us to comprehend the emotional effects of our decisions and behaviors on them.

4. Accept Accountability: The cornerstone of accountability is self-awareness. It nudges us to accept

accountability for our choices and the outcomes—past and present—of those choices.

Learning to Be Self-Aware

Self-awareness cultivation is a lifetime endeavor that calls for endurance, self-compassion, and dedication. It uses a variety of methods and procedures, such as:

1. Meditation and mindful journaling are two mindfulness techniques that might help us become more aware of our thoughts and feelings.

2. Self-Reflection: Taking regular breaks to reflect and write in a journal enables us to discover our inner selves.

3. Requesting Feedback: We can learn a lot about our blind spots by asking dependable friends, family members, or professionals for their honest opinions.

4. Working with a therapist can be helpful in developing greater self-awareness, particularly when tackling complex problems like narcissism.

The Way Ahead

Self-awareness is the driving force behind the change in the setting of maternal narcissism. It is the knowledge that we have the ability to change, to free ourselves from negative habits, and to foster better relationships with our kids.

Let's keep in mind that self-awareness is not a destination but rather a companion on this journey of self-discovery. It is a light that constantly directs us in the direction of personal development, increased empathy, and the achievement of our full potential as devoted and supportive moms. It is, in fact, the lighthouse that guides us along this profound path of comprehension, restoration, and promotion of good relationships

CHAPTER 2

The Narcissistic Temperament

A Multifaced Nature of a Complex Trait: Different Facets of Narcissism

The word "narcissism" carries a significant meaning and frequently conjures up pictures of self-indulgence, vanity, and egotism. Narcissism is not a single, all-encompassing idea; rather, it is a multidimensional trait that exists on a continuum, similar to many psychological disorders. In the book "Am I a Narcissistic Mother? Understanding, Healing, and Nurturing Healthy Relationships," which will examine the various characteristics of narcissism and their implications for maternal conduct, it is very important to comprehend these various facets.

What causes narcissism?

Exploring the causes of narcissism is crucial to understanding its many features. Narcissism is frequently a result of complicated interactions between one's genetics, environment, and life events rather than just being a personality trait.

Magnificent narcissism

The Spotlight Craver: Grandiose narcissism, at one extreme of the spectrum, is defined by an exaggerated feeling of self-importance, a continual desire for adulation, and a propensity to exaggerate accomplishments. The egotistical narcissist frequently seeks attention and rules conversations with tales of their successes.

Maternal Implications: For a mother who exhibits grandiose narcissistic characteristics, motherhood may turn into a platform to highlight her accomplishments or live vicariously via her children's successes. This may result in her being less sensitive to the emotional needs of her kids.

Narcissism that is vulnerable

The Fragile Ego: On the other end of the spectrum is weak narcissism, characterized by a pervasive sense of insecurity, an extreme sensitivity to criticism, and a propensity to victimize others. The weak narcissist frequently presents a facade of modesty while harboring deep self-doubt.

Maternal Implications: Due to her own emotional brittleness, a mother with sensitive narcissistic features may find it difficult to support her children emotionally. Her children may experience an oppressive environment as a result of her desire for frequent reassurance.

Localized narcissism

The Benevolent Martyr: A distinctive aspect of communal narcissism is the belief that one is extraordinarily charitable, selfless, and morally superior.

They frequently base their sense of self-worth on their perceived goodness and selflessness.

Maternal Implications: A mother who exhibits communal narcissistic traits may prioritize self-sacrifice for her kids, but this may come at the expense of boundaries and uniqueness. She could anticipate that her kids will live up to her idealized concept of the ideal family.

Subtle narcissism

The Hidden Manipulator: Covert narcissism manifests as an outward gesture of altruism and humility while hiding ulterior motives and manipulative tendencies. To further their agenda, covert narcissists frequently resort to guilt and emotional blackmail.

Maternal Implications: A mother who exhibits hidden narcissistic features may use deceptive methods to keep her children under control. To satisfy her wants, she might emotionally blackmail or guilt-trip them.

Effects on Mothers' Behavior

For mothers who wonder whether they possess narcissistic traits, it is imperative to comprehend these various aspects of narcissism. It enables a comprehensive self-evaluation and aids them in identifying the precise characteristics that might be influencing their parenting style. Additionally, it highlights that narcissism is a complex interplay of different traits rather than an all-or-nothing attribute.

To begin the process of healing and personal development, one must first recognize these aspects of themselves. It provides the chance to change one's conduct, look for counseling or support, and ultimately develop better relationships with one's kids. It serves as a reminder that change is possible and that empathy, self-awareness, and transformation may flourish even in the complex world of narcissism.

Extremes against Milder Traits: The Narcistic Spectrum

The word "narcissism" conjures up a spectrum of actions and characteristics that go from the worst to the best. This aspect of human nature touches on self-love and self-centeredness, and it can take many different forms. In the context of the book "Am I a Narcissistic Mother? Understanding, Healing, and Nurturing Healthy Relationships," it's critical to examine the subtle differences between these extremes and milder narcissistic tendencies in order to acquire a thorough grasp of the complicated phenomena.

Grandiose narcissism is one of the extremes

Grandiose narcissism is at the far end of the narcissistic continuum. This feature is frequently distinguished by:

1. An excessive belief in their own importance characterizes grandiose narcissists. In a variety of spheres of life, such as intelligence, attractiveness, or achievement, they feel they are superior to others.

2. Constant Need for Admiration: Grandiose narcissists always seek the approval of others. They are constantly looking for attention, and if they don't get it, they could get angry.

3. Lack of Empathy: Grandiose narcissists struggle to feel empathy for others. They frequently see people as tools to help them achieve their goals and struggle to understand or relate to the needs and emotions of others.

4. Exploitative Behavior: Manipulating and taking advantage of others are prevalent characteristics. Grandiose narcissists may take advantage of people to further their objectives without giving the victims' welfare any thought.

Vulnerable narcissism is one of the milder traits

Milder narcissistic characteristics, frequently linked to fragile narcissism, can be found on the other end of the continuum. Among these qualities are:

1. Insecurity: Vulnerable narcissists frequently struggle with self-doubt and a shaky sense of their own value. As opposed to their opulent peers, they may conceal their arrogance under a façade of humility.

2. Sensitivity to Criticism: For narcissists who are open to criticism, even positive input, it can be extremely upsetting. They may respond in a defensive manner or by withdrawing.

3. Fear of Abandonment: Members of this group frequently have deep-seated anxiety about being rejected or abandoned, which can manifest as clingy or dependent behaviors in romantic relationships.

4. Self-Deprecation: In order to hide their actual sense of entitlement and superiority, vulnerable narcissists may adopt a self-deprecating attitude.

Implications for Maternal Behavior in Spectrum Navigation

For mothers who are on a self-discovery journey, especially those who are unsure if they display narcissistic tendencies, understanding the difference between the extremes and lesser features of narcissism is essential. It serves as a reminder that narcissism is a spectrum-like quality rather than a one-size-fits-all characteristic.

The extreme end of the scale for moms with grandiose narcissistic tendencies can result in actions that are especially destructive to their kids, such as emotional neglect or manipulation. It is crucial for the mother's and her family's wellbeing to recognize these severe qualities.

On the other hand, mothers who exhibit weaker narcissistic traits—often resulting from vulnerability—may have trouble boosting their self-esteem and managing stress. Support and counseling may help these mothers deal with their defensiveness and worries about desertion.

The narcissistic trait spectrum serves as a reminder that human behavior is complicated and that different levels of narcissism can be present in different people. Particularly in the context of maternal responsibilities, identifying where one stands on this spectrum is a crucial first step toward personal development and healthy relationships. It emphasizes the capacity for adjustment, self-awareness, and the development of understanding and empathy within the context of the family dynamic.

The Origin of a Complex Trait: How Neglect Develops

The process of narcissistic growth is fascinating and complex, including a variety of psychological, social, and environmental elements. In this essay, we will examine the multidimensional path of narcissism's development. Understanding how narcissism takes root and flourishes is vital, especially in the context of the book "Am I a Narcissistic Mother? Understanding, Healing, and Nurturing Healthy Relationships."

Childhood influences: The Early Root

Narcissism frequently has its origins in interactions and experiences from early life. Early influences like these can pave the way for the emergence of narcissistic characteristics.

Parental Influences: Parents are crucial in influencing how their children view themselves. Parenting that is too indulgent or careless can encourage the emergence of narcissistic traits. For instance, a child who receives excessive praise and is never held responsible for their behavior may develop an exaggerated sense of entitlement as they get older.

Emotional Validation: Children who do not receive enough emotional support and validation may seek it from outside sources to make up for it. Later in life, this may appear as a continual desire for praise and affirmation.

Childhood trauma: As a coping technique, traumatic events like physical or emotional abuse can cause the development of narcissistic tendencies. Narcissism can act as a barrier to block out the hurt from previous trauma.

Societal influences as a cultural factor

The community and culture in which a person is raised can also influence how narcissistic traits emerge.

Cultural values: Narcissistic traits may be cultivated in societies that value individualism, rivalry, and material achievement. Self-promotion and selfishness may be rewarded in such settings.

Social media and technology: These developments have made narcissistic behavior more prevalent. For those who are vulnerable, the constant search for approval through likes and comments can feed narcissistic tendencies.

Celebrity Culture: The exaltation of celebrities and their opulent lifestyles can encourage narcissistic tendencies in people and inspire them to strive for lofty goals.

Behavioral Strategies for Dealing with Vulnerability

Narcissism frequently emerges as a coping strategy to deal with emotions of inadequacy and vulnerability. People may act in narcissistic ways to protect themselves from these perceived weaknesses:

Self-Enhancement: In order to increase their self-esteem, people may use self-enhancement techniques. Exaggerating accomplishments, pursuing unceasing adoration, and downplaying failures are a few examples of this.

Denial of Vulnerability: In order to shield themselves from emotional anguish, narcissists frequently repress or deny feelings of vulnerability while creating an image of invulnerability and superiority.

Idealized Self-Image: To avoid their genuine, more frail selves, narcissists may develop an idealized picture of themselves.

Adverse Life Events' Function in Activating Narcissistic Traits

Negative life situations can operate as triggers that bring these tendencies to the fore, while childhood experiences and cultural variables also play a role in the development of narcissism.

Significant loss or failure can set off narcissistic tendencies as people fight to maintain their sense of self-worth and identity.

Relationship difficulties: When people experience relationship difficulties or feel as though their self-worth is in danger, narcissistic qualities can become more evident.

Stress and pressure: Narcissistic inclinations can be made worse by high-stress circumstances and the pressure to meet impossible standards.

The emergence of narcissism is the result of a complex interplay of influences from early life, cultural context, psychological mechanisms, and traumatic experiences. It is a multidimensional quality that might appear in different ways, rather than a universal phenomenon. For those starting a road of self-discovery and personal growth, especially those wondering whether they have narcissistic traits as moms, understanding these developmental elements is crucial. In order to confront and manage these complicated roots and their impact on maternal behavior and family dynamics, it is important to have self-awareness, empathy, and therapeutic assistance.

CHAPTER 3

Understanding the symptoms

Introspection and Self-Examination: Self-Discovery Mirrors

Few methods are as powerful and transformative in the pursuit of self-awareness and personal progress as introspection and self-examination. Our deepest thoughts, feelings, and behaviors are reflected in these two mirrors of self-discovery, allowing us to examine the complex fabric of our being. In the context of the book "Am I a Narcissistic Mother? Understanding, Healing, and Nurturing Healthy Relationships," self-reflection and introspection are essential practices that hold the promise of significant change.

Definition of Introspection and Self-Examination

Although the terms "self-examination" and "introspection" are frequently used interchangeably, they refer to different kinds of self-awareness.

Examining oneself critically involves paying serious attention to one's thoughts, deeds, and beliefs. In order to understand our character and values, it entails challenging our actions, decisions, and motivations.

Self-reflection that is deeper and more meditative is known as introspection. It explores the fundamental motivations, wants, and feelings that influence our choices and actions. It's like looking into the motivations behind our actions.

The Influence of Self-Reflection

Through self-examination, which functions as a magnifying glass, we can:

1. Recognize Patterns: We can spot repeating themes and tendencies by closely examining our actions and cognitive processes. Understanding how narcissistic

tendencies may appear in our behaviors and interactions depends on our ability to recognize them.

2. Assess Impact: Self-examination enables us to determine how our actions affect other people, particularly our children. It aids in our understanding of the emotional effects of our actions.

3. Determine Triggers: We are able to identify the circumstances or triggers that result in narcissistic conduct. Finding these triggers—whether they are related to stress, insecurity, or particular situations—is the first step towards managing them

4. Self-examination cultivates accountability by enabling us to accept responsibility for our choices and the results of those choices. It acknowledges our autonomy over our actions and decisions.

The Depths of Self-Examination

On the other side, introspection explores our interior emotional landscape.

1. Understanding Motivations: Through introspection, we can learn what drives our actions. Are we looking for approval, power, or a feeling of superiority? Change requires an understanding of these reasons.

2. Exploring weaknesses: Introspection pushes us to face our anxieties, insecurities, and weaknesses. Examining the causes of our narcissistic inclinations demands courage.

3. Fostering Empathy: Through introspection, we can foster empathy by becoming aware of both our own and other people's feelings. It enables us to understand our children's wants and feelings by observing the world through their eyes.

4. Self-Compassion Cultivation: One way to develop self-compassion is through introspection. It entails accepting our flaws and forgiving ourselves for previous transgressions, opening the door for personal development.

The road ahead

Examining oneself and reflecting on one's life are not endeavors for the weak of heart. They call for bravery, openness, and a dedication to growth. For moms negotiating the difficulties of narcissism, in particular, they are transformative processes that offer healing and growth.

Let us embrace the mirrors of self-examination and introspection as vital tools as we go out on the voyage of self-discovery within the world of maternal narcissism. They serve as the compass that leads us through the maze of our own psyche, illuminating its dark corners and providing a way to comprehend, heal, and foster better relationships with our kids. It is a journey that starts inside of ourselves, and it may be there that we discover the secrets to achieving great personal change.

Common Narcissistic Behaviors: Unveiling The Complex Web of Self-Centered Actions

A complex personality trait with a spectrum of manifestations, narcissism can take many different forms. The interactions and relationships of people who have narcissistic tendencies are shaped by these behaviors, which are frequently motivated by a deep-seated need for approval and self-importance.

Narcissistic Behaviors: Definition

Prior to examining particular acts, it's crucial to comprehend the fundamental traits that characterize narcissism:

Grandiosity: Narcissists frequently exhibit an overinflated sense of their own importance. They might think they are better than others in a variety of ways, including intelligence, prosperity, or beauty.

Need for Admiration: People who have narcissistic tendencies always crave attention and approval. They look for outside validation to support their flimsy self-esteem.

Lack of Empathy: Narcissists frequently lack empathy. They find it difficult to relate to or comprehend the emotions and needs of others, seeing them only as resources to help them achieve their goals.

Manipulation: Narcissists may use deception and exploitation to further their agendas without caring about the welfare of the people they take advantage of.

Typical Narcissistic Acts

Let's examine some typical narcissistic behaviors while keeping these fundamental traits in mind:

Narcissists frequently put their own needs, wants, and feelings ahead of those of others out of self-centeredness. They might dominate talks, making them mostly about themselves, and show no interest in hearing other people's opinions.

Continual Need for Validation: Narcissists have an unquenchable thirst for approval. They frequently look for external affirmation, and if they don't get it, they could get angry or hurt.

Manipulative Techniques: Narcissistic behavior is characterized by manipulation. This may involve guilt-tripping, emotional blackmail, or exploiting others.

Lack of Accountability: Narcissists frequently find it difficult to accept accountability for their deeds. They could deny guilt, assign responsibility to others, or downplay the consequences of their actions.

Exploitative behavior: Narcissists may take advantage of people to satisfy their own demands, with no regard for the welfare of those they are taking advantage of. This can show up in a number of ways, such as by abusing someone's kindness or emotional support.

Sense of Entitlement: Narcissism frequently coexists with a pervasive sense of entitlement. Narcissists could think they have earned special treatment, advantages, or recognition.

Fragile Self-Esteem: Ironically, many narcissists conceal fragile self-esteem behind a show of grandeur. They are extremely sensitive to criticism, and when their self-worth is in jeopardy, they may respond defensively or angrily.

Idealization and Devaluation: Narcissists frequently vacillate between idealization and devaluation in romantic relationships. When their expectations are not realized, they may begin by idealizing someone and lavishing them with love and admiration, but this idealization can swiftly develop into devaluation.

Effect on Motherly Roles

These actions can have a significant impact on moms who exhibit narcissistic tendencies in their parenting roles. Having a narcissistic mother can cause emotional neglect, manipulation, and a lack of emotional awareness in children. A child's emotional needs could be neglected in favor of the demand for constant approval and validation, which could have long-term emotional repercussions.

The complicated web of self-centered acts that are founded on the desire for approval and self-importance gives rise to common narcissistic tendencies. For people who are on a path of self-discovery within the setting of parental narcissism, recognizing these behaviors is crucial. It emphasizes the value of self-awareness, treatment, and support in dealing with and minimizing these behaviors to promote healthier family relationships. Although narcissism has many facets, it is not an insurmountable barrier to the development of empathy and understanding, as well as transformation and progress.

A Crucial Compass for the Journey of Self-Discovery: Seeking Honest Feedback

The pursuit of truthful criticism acts as a compass on the winding path of self-discovery and personal development. Asking for honest criticism is a sign of humility and self-awareness since it acknowledges that we are fallible and that other people's viewpoints can provide priceless insights.

The Influence of Direct Criticism

Sincere criticism serves as a mirror that others hold up for us, reflecting back to us elements of ourselves that we might not immediately notice. It has several crucial characteristics, including:

1. Objectivity: Sincere criticism offers a dispassionate assessment of our actions and their effects. It removes the lenses of self-perception, enabling us to perceive ourselves through others' perspectives.

2. It provides insights into how our behavior affects people around us, particularly our kids. It displays the emotional repercussions of our actions, whether they are good or bad.

3. Seeking truthful criticism encourages self-reflection. It challenges us to reflect on our intentions, deeds, and cognitive processes, fostering increased self-awareness.

4. Growth: Even constructive criticism offers room for personal development. It draws attention to areas where we may enhance, modify, or adjust our behavior.

The Willingness to Seek Recommendation

Requesting frank feedback can be a difficult endeavor. It necessitates openness, modesty, and a readiness to accept unsettling information. Taking into account the following points can help you get genuine feedback:

Choose Reliable Confidants: Ask for input from someone you know will have your best interests in mind and can provide insightful criticism.

Be open and receptive. Approach feedback with an open mind and an eagerness to hear what others have to say. Avoid defending yourself or being disrespectful.

Pose Specific Questions: Ask specific questions regarding your behaviors or activities rather than broad remarks. You might ask, "How do you think I handle stress in our family?" as an example.

Encourage Honesty: Make it known that you appreciate honesty and are receptive to both positive and constructive criticism. Make it safe for people to freely express their opinions.

Dealing with Criticism as a Mother

The importance of getting open feedback increases while discussing parental roles. Being a mother is an intensely intimate experience where our actions have a big impact on our kids. We can learn a lot about our parenting style and its effects from our children, partners, or close friends and family.

Children's opinions can be very instructive for mothers who wonder whether they have narcissistic tendencies. Children can offer frank insights into their experiences within the family dynamic since they are frequently sensitive to subtle emotional cues.

In the context of maternal roles, specifically, seeking honest feedback is a compass that directs us on the path to self-improvement and stronger relationships. It is a brave and self-aware act, an admission that learning comes from both within and outside of us.

Let's keep in mind that criticism, even when it's uncomfortable, is a gift that can help us become more self-aware and change our behaviors as we negotiate the challenging terrain of parenthood and narcissism. It is evidence of our dedication to raising families with healthier relationships and developing into the greatest mothers and people we can be.

CHAPTER 4

The Effects on Your Children

Maternal Narcissism's Effect On Children's Emotional Consequences

Children's emotional health is closely related to how well they get along with their parents, especially their moms. When maternal narcissism is involved, it can have a significant impact on a child's emotional growth.

The Value of Mother-Child Bonding

One of a person's most important relationships in life is their relationship with their mother. It influences a child's sense of self, emotional fortitude, and capacity to develop positive relationships in the future. But a narcissistic mother can damage this crucial bond in a number of ways:

Narcissistic women could be concerned with their own demands and desires, leaving little emotional room for their kids. The youngster may have feelings of abandonment and inadequateness as a result of this emotional neglect.

Constant Affection: Narcissistic mothers may go between lavishly showing affection to their kids and abruptly withholding it. The youngster may become confused and uneasy as a result of this inconsistency.

Lack of Empathy: People with narcissistic tendencies frequently lack empathy. Children with narcissistic mothers may have feelings of loneliness as a result of not having their emotions acknowledged or understood.

To influence their children's conduct, narcissistic mothers may use emotional manipulation techniques like gaslighting or guilt-tripping. A child's confidence in themselves and self-worth may suffer as a result of this manipulation.

Parentification: Reversing the parent-child relationship, some narcissistic women may rely on their kids for emotional support. This parentification may subject the youngster to emotional strain beyond their years and adult responsibilities.

The Effects of Emotion on Children

The emotional repercussions for children of narcissistic moms can be severe and long-lasting.

Low Self-Esteem: Constant criticism or the conviction that their needs are insignificant might cause children to develop low self-esteem.

Anxiety and despair: Children who experience anxiety and despair may do so due to the emotional turbulence in their families. They can internalize the anxiety and confusion they are experiencing.

Trust Issues: In the parent-child connection, a lack of emotional constancy and empathy can lead to trust issues. Future attachment issues for children could arise.

Guilt and Shame: Narcissistic mothers' manipulation techniques can make children feel guilty and ashamed even when they are not at fault.

Repetition of Patterns: Narcissistic moms' offspring may unintentionally continue unhealthy relationship patterns in their own adult relationships.

The Recovery Procedure

It is crucial to understand that maternal narcissism's emotional effects are not predetermined. Growth and healing are attainable. The following actions can help in this process:

Self-awareness: Be aware of the negative effects of your mother's narcissism on your emotional health. The first step to recovery is self-awareness.

Seek Support: Speak with a therapist or support group that focuses on recovering from narcissistic abuse. Speaking with a sympathetic ear can be quite helpful.

Set limits: If at all feasible, establish healthy limits with your mother in particular. Boundaries safeguard your emotional health.

Give self-care and self-compassion a priority. Take care of your emotional wellbeing by engaging in peaceful and therapeutic activities and practices.

Although there are considerable emotional repercussions for children of narcissistic moms, these effects do not determine a child's destiny. Emotional resilience and healing are reachable objectives with self-awareness, assistance, and self-care. To create healthier relationships with oneself and others, one must take the brave step of escaping the emotional bonds of parental narcissism. It serves as evidence of the human spirit's steadfastness and adaptability.

Repercussions for Their Self-Esteem

The dynamics of the family, particularly the mother-child bond, can have a significant impact on self-esteem, the cornerstone of a healthy self-identity. This delicate balance can be upset by maternal narcissism, which can have long-lasting effects on a child's self-esteem.

The importance of self-esteem

A person's life is significantly shaped by their feeling of self-worth, which is frequently referred to as self-respect. It affects one's self-perception, social interactions, and capacity for resilience in the face of difficulties. The development of self-esteem in childhood is primarily influenced by the mother-child bond, making the maternal figure's function crucial.

Effects of Maternal Narcissism on Self-Esteem

A child's self-esteem can be severely impacted by a mother's narcissism in a number of ways:

Constant Criticism: Narcissistic mothers may be overly critical of their kids, posing impossible expectations and undermining their self-esteem. Such situations can cause children to internalize the idea that they are never good enough.

Emotional Neglect: Narcissistic mothers may neglect their children emotionally because they are too focused on their own requirements. The youngster may experience feelings of worthlessness and emotional desertion as a result of this emotional void.

Need for Validation: Because their self-esteem is so strongly linked to other people's perceptions, children of narcissistic mothers may develop a lifelong need for outside validation and approval.

Consistency: Narcissistic mothers may alternate between showing affection and withholding it, which makes their children's emotional environments unpredictable. Feelings of insecurity may be exacerbated by this inconsistency.

Gaslighting and emotional manipulation are two techniques that narcissistic moms may use to manipulate their kids. This manipulation has the potential to skew a child's understanding of reality and erode their self-confidence.

Fear of Rejection: Children who grow up with narcissistic mothers may experience fear of abandonment and rejection, which makes it difficult for them to create meaningful relationships in the future.

The long-term effect

Children's self-esteem can be negatively impacted by narcissistic mothers far into adulthood.

Low Self-Esteem: Narcissistic mothers often leave their children with low self-esteem that lasts far into adulthood. They might keep doubting their value and skill.

Perfectionism: People with perfectionistic inclinations feel pressure to do well in all areas of life to demonstrate their value. This tendency can be brought on by a persistent need for acceptance and a fear of criticism.

Setting boundaries is hard. People who struggle to set appropriate boundaries as adults are more susceptible to manipulation and exploitation in their relationships. Lack of boundaries in childhood might cause this problem.

Recovery and Healing: It's critical to understand that self-esteem may be nourished and rebuilt over time. The healing process can be facilitated by therapy, self-care routines, and strong social networks.

The narcissism of a mother can have a significant negative effect on a child's sense of self-worth, self-trust, and general mental health. Understanding how mother narcissism affects one's self-esteem is an essential first step toward rehabilitation. The ability of individuals to go on a journey of self-discovery and self-compassion, which ultimately fosters greater self-esteem and a more profound sense of self-worth, is a monument to the perseverance of the human spirit.

Impact on Cognition and Behavior

The complicated and frequently deeply ingrained personality trait of maternal narcissism can have a significant impact on a child's cognitive and behavioral growth. Children face a variety of obstacles as they make their way through the complex maze of maternal narcissism, which affects both how they see the world and how they behave in it.

How Maternal Narcissism Shapes Thought: The Cognitive Lens

A child's cognitive development can be severely impacted by a mother's narcissism.

skewed self-perception: Narcissistic women who nurture their children may have skewed views of themselves. They could internalize unfavorable or inaccurate perceptions of themselves and have the notion that they are never good enough.

Children who don't receive adequate emotional validation from their mothers may become heavily dependent on external affirmation. They might develop a strong preference for seeking affirmation from others in order to boost their self-esteem.

Fear of Rejection: Narcissistic parenting can cause children to harbor a deep-seated fear of being rejected and abandoned. Any criticism or rejection may be interpreted by children as a threat to their sense of value.

When their mother's actions and words are inconsistent, children may struggle with cognitive dissonance and have conflicting beliefs and feelings. This may cause uncertainty and self-doubt.

Development of Coping Mechanisms: Children may acquire coping skills like people-pleasing, perfectionism, or conflict avoidance in order to manage the emotional upheaval brought on by their narcissistic mothers.

The Behavioral Consequences: How Maternal Narcissism Influences Behavior

Additionally, having a significant impact on a child's behavioral habits is a mother's narcissism.

People-Pleasing: Young children may act in ways that appeal to others in an effort to win their mother's approval and fend off criticism. This can set up a habit where they put other people's needs before their own.

Perfectionism: Children who feel the need to show their worth may develop into perfectionists who pursue excellence in all facets of life. A strong motivator can be the fear of failing.

Lack of Boundaries: A child's capacity to establish appropriate boundaries may be compromised by a narcissistic mother. They can find it difficult to stand up for themselves or safeguard their own mental wellbeing.

Maternal narcissism can create an environment that is inconsistent and emotionally unstable, which can make it difficult to trust other people. Children could develop a guarded and circumspect approach to relationships.

Pattern Repetition: Without assistance, kids raised by narcissistic moms could unintentionally repeat unhealthy relationship patterns in their own adult relationships.

The Recovery Procedure

It's crucial to understand that healing and transformation are possible, even if maternal narcissism can have a significant negative impact on cognition and behavior.

Self-awareness: The first step toward change is recognizing the cognitive and behavioral patterns affected by parental narcissism.

Therapy and Support: Attending therapy sessions or joining a support group can give you vital skills for recovery and the development of better thought and behavior patterns.

Setting Boundaries: To interrupt negative behavioral cycles, it's crucial to learn how to set and maintain healthy boundaries.

Self-Compassion: Developing self-compassion is essential for restoring self-esteem and promoting more positive thought patterns.

A complex and permanent component of a child's development is the impact of a narcissistic mother on their cognitive and behavioral development. It affects how they perceive themselves, relate to others, and move through the world. It's not a life sentence, though. People who were reared in the shadow of mother narcissism can modify their cognitive and behavioral patterns, eventually cultivating healthy relationships with themselves and others, if they have self-awareness, support, and the courage to begin a journey of healing.

It is evidence of the tenacity, adaptability, and progress of the human soul.

CHAPTER 5

Navigating the Blame Game

The complicated and frequently profoundly ingrained personality trait of maternal narcissism can hang over a child's life like a crushing cloud of shame. One significant component of the complex dynamics in such households is the guilt trap, a persistent emotional web spun by narcissistic moms.

Defined: The Guilt Trap

Narcissistic mothers use the guilt trap as a cunning tactic to emotionally manipulate and control their kids. It entails teaching remorse and responsibility to the child and making the child feel obligated to the mother. One of the guilt trap's main components is:

Emotional Manipulation: To control their child's behavior and emotions, narcissistic mothers may use emotional manipulation techniques, including guilt-tripping, humiliating, or playing the victim.

Obligation: Young children are frequently taught to feel that they must fulfill their mother's emotional demands at the price of their own happiness and aspirations.

Fear of Abandonment: The guilt trap takes advantage of the child's weakness and exploits their fear of abandonment to maintain control and compliance.

Conditional Love: Narcissistic mothers may withhold affection or approval, giving it only when the child does as they are told. The child experiences an emotional rollercoaster as a result of this conditional affection.

The Guilt Trap's Emotional Chokehold

The child is under the profound emotional control of the guilt trap.

Constant Anxiety: Children caught in the guilt trap experience constant anxiety because they worry that every choice they make may enrage their mother and set off her guilt-inducing strategies.

Eroded Self-Esteem: The guilt trap causes a child to internalize feelings of inadequacy and the notion that they will never be good enough to live up to their mother's standards, which erodes the child's sense of self-worth.

Dependence: Children who look to their mother's praise and validation as a source of self-worth may grow emotionally dependent on it.

Difficulty Setting Boundaries: The guilt trap can make it difficult for kids to set and uphold appropriate boundaries because they worry about the emotional repercussions.

How to Escape the Guilt Trap

For children of narcissistic mothers, escaping the guilt trap is a difficult but necessary journey.

Self-awareness: The first step to freedom is realizing the emotional effects of the guilt trap.

Setting Boundaries: Learning to establish and uphold appropriate boundaries is essential for escaping the emotional grip of the guilt trap.

Seeking Support: Therapy or support groups can provide you with the tools and direction you need to recover from the emotional scars the guilt trap has caused.

Rebuilding Self-Esteem: In order to end the cycle of guilt and emotional manipulation, it is crucial to cultivate self-worth and self-compassion.

A pernicious manifestation of parental narcissism that has a powerful emotional hold over a child's life is the guilt trap. It is not, however, an inevitable fate. Those who are caught in the guilt trap can set out on a road of emotional emancipation with self-awareness, boundary-setting, support, and the will to escape. It serves as a tribute to the human spirit's tenacity, capacity for recovery, and potential for development, opening the door to healthier relationships and a more promising emotional future.

Difference Setting Between Accountability and Self-Blame

Making the distinction between accountability and self-blame is crucial in the complicated world of personal development and healing. Although they both entail accepting accountability for one's choices and the results, they have very different effects on one's mental and emotional health.

Taking Responsibility: The Road to Empowerment

The idea of accountability is positive and powerful. It entails accepting responsibility for one's deeds, choices, and results without blaming or judging oneself. Important accountability factors include:

Accountability: People who embrace accountability accept responsibility for their deeds and are aware that their decisions have an impact.

Learning: Accountability is a process that emphasizes growth. It entails being prepared to change course after making a mistake and learning from it.

Empowerment: Adopting accountability equips people to make positive changes in their relationships and personal lives. It is a proactive move toward personal development.

Respect for Healthy Boundaries: Accountability respects healthy boundaries by acknowledging that people are only accountable for their own actions and not those of others or their feelings.

The destructive spiral: self-accusation

On the other side, self-blame is a negative thought pattern that is disabling. It entails placing a disproportionate amount of blame, shame, or responsibility on oneself for undesirable results or circumstances, frequently without justification. Self-blame's main components include:

Abundant Guilt Even in circumstances where one's actions or decisions were not the main cause of the issue, self-blame is marked by intense feelings of guilt and humiliation.

Disempowerment: Self-blame causes people to feel powerless and burdened by their perceived failings.

Negative Self-Image: As people repeatedly criticize themselves for their perceived errors, self-blame erodes self-esteem and self-worth.

Unhealthy Responsibility: Self-blame entails taking on an excessive amount of accountability for the feelings and deeds of others, even when this is not justified.

Taking Care of the Fine Line

Although it might be difficult, distinguishing between accountability and self-blame is essential for emotional healing and personal development.

Self-Reflection: During this process, self-reflection is a useful tool. It entails critically assessing one's behavior and choices, admitting areas that require improvement, and doing so without engaging in excessive self-criticism.

Seeking Perspective: Getting feedback from close friends, family members, or a therapist can offer an objective viewpoint and assist people in determining if they are taking responsibility or succumbing to self-blame.

Forgiveness: A key component of recovery is learning to forgive oneself for errors and mishaps. It entails accepting flaws and exercising self-compassion.

Setting limits: Healthy limits must be established and upheld in order to avoid self-blame. The key is understanding where one's obligation ends and that of others begins.

Separating responsibility from self-blame is a crucial part of recovery, particularly for people affected by maternal narcissism. Accepting accountability enables people to take responsibility for their choices and grow from their experiences, which promotes personal development. However, self-blame is a negative habit that degrades well-being and self-esteem.

Genuine healing and transformation depend on striking the correct balance between responsibility and self-compassion. It is a credit to the human spirit's tenacity that it can successfully navigate the difficulties of self-awareness and self-improvement while cultivating a compassionate and understanding connection with oneself.

Forgiveness and Self-Compassion

Two strong and transformational forces—self-compassion and forgiveness—emerge in the complex process of recovering from the wounds caused by parental narcissism. These two emotional healing pillars provide consolation and a road to inner peace, ultimately opening the door to better relationships and a happier emotional future.

Self-Compassion: Taking Care of Your Inner Needs

The act of treating oneself with the same consideration, compassion, and understanding that one would extend to a close friend through a trying period is known as self-compassion. There are numerous crucial elements in it:

Self-Kindness: Rather than harsh self-criticism or judgment, self-compassion calls for treating oneself with warmth and gentleness.

Common Humanity: Self-compassion makes people aware that they are not alone in their challenges by acknowledging that suffering and imperfection are common experiences.

Mindfulness: A crucial component of self-compassion is mindfulness. It entails embracing one's sentiments without passing judgment on them.

Because it combats the constant self-criticism and feelings of inadequacy that narcissistic moms frequently implant in their children, self-compassion is particularly effective in healing the wounds of parental narcissism. It gives people the emotional support they might have lacked when they were young.

Release from Resentment through Forgiveness

When one forgives, they are freeing themselves from the load of resentment and wrath that can weigh heavy on their hearts. Forgiveness is frequently mistaken for endorsing or excusing harsh behavior. The essential components of forgiveness are:

Letting Go: Forgiveness is letting go of the need for vengeance or retaliation as well as the emotional attachments to old grudges.

Healing: It is a process of healing that enables people to achieve emotional liberation, closure, and peace.

Empowerment: The decision to forgive is an empowering one. It shows that a person is in charge of their emotions and is no longer letting the agony of the past govern their present.

It's important to remember that forgiving a narcissistic mother involves releasing oneself from the emotional bonds of the past, not accepting her actions. It is a profoundly individual decision that gives people the power to restore their emotional health.

Self-compassion and forgiveness Work Together

Self-compassion and forgiveness are complementary ideas that support one another in the healing process.

Self-Compassion Promotes Forgiveness: Self-compassion promotes self-acceptance and emotional healing, which cultivates a favorable environment for forgiveness.

Self-Compassion is Enhanced by Forgiveness: Self-compassion is strengthened by forgiveness, which promotes inner serenity and self-acceptance.

When a mother is narcissistic, self-compassion and forgiveness are powerful drivers for recovery. They give people the emotional support and independence they require to free themselves from the bonds of the past and forge stronger bonds with others. The healing process is evidence of how resilient the human spirit is, able to find comfort and fortitude even in the most trying situations.

Forgiveness and Self-Compassion

Two potent and transforming forces stand out in the complex process of healing, especially for individuals affected by the difficulties of maternal narcissism: self-compassion and forgiveness. These two emotional healing pillars provide consolation and a road to inner peace, ultimately opening the door to better relationships and a happier emotional future.

Self-Compassion: Taking Care of Yourself

The act of treating oneself with the same consideration, compassion, and understanding that one would extend to a close friend through a trying period is known as self-compassion. There are numerous crucial elements in it:

Self-Kindness: Rather than harsh self-criticism or judgment, self-compassion calls for treating oneself with warmth and gentleness.

Common Humanity: Self-compassion makes people aware that they are not alone in their challenges by acknowledging that suffering and imperfection are common experiences.

Mindfulness: A crucial component of self-compassion is mindfulness. It entails embracing one's sentiments without passing judgment on them.

Because it combats the constant self-criticism and feelings of inadequacy that frequently follow such experiences, self-compassion is particularly effective in healing the wounds of mother narcissism. It gives people the emotional support they might have lacked when they were young.

Release from Resentment through Forgiveness

When one forgives, they are freeing themselves from the load of resentment and wrath that can weigh heavy on their hearts. Forgiveness is frequently mistaken for endorsing or excusing harsh behavior. The essential components of forgiveness are:

Letting Go: Forgiveness is letting go of the need for vengeance or retaliation as well as the emotional attachments to old grudges.

Healing: It is a process of healing that enables people to achieve emotional liberation, closure, and peace.

Being empowered It is empowering to choose forgiveness. It shows that a person is in charge of their emotions and is no longer letting the agony of the past govern their present.

It's important to remember that forgiving a narcissistic mother involves releasing oneself from the emotional bonds of the past, not accepting her actions. It is a profoundly individual decision that gives people the power to restore their emotional health.

Self-compassion and forgiveness Work Together

Self-compassion and forgiveness are complementary ideas that support one another in the healing process.

Forgiveness Is Fostered by Self-Compassion: Self-compassion fosters emotional healing and self-acceptance, which prepare the way for forgiveness.

Self-Compassion is Strengthened by Forgiveness: Self-compassion is strengthened because forgiveness of oneself and others promotes inner calm and self-acceptance.

When a mother is narcissistic, self-compassion and forgiveness are powerful drivers for recovery. They give people the emotional support and independence they require to free themselves from the bonds of the past and forge stronger bonds with others. The healing process is evidence of how resilient the human spirit is, able to find comfort and fortitude even in the most trying situations.

CHAPTER 6

Recovering and Transforming

Development Strategies for Personal

Personal development is a continuous process of self-actualization, self-improvement, and self-discovery that lasts a lifetime. It entails making a deliberate effort to increase one's emotional health, knowledge, and skills, which will ultimately result in a life that is more meaningful and rewarding.

Self-Awareness: The Basis for Development

Self-awareness is the basis for personal development. It entails a thorough and frank analysis of your ideas, emotions, behaviors, and motivations. Self-awareness-improving techniques include:

Mindfulness Practice: To improve your awareness of your inner experiences, try mindfulness meditation or other mindfulness practices.

Journaling: By recording your thoughts and feelings in a journal, you might see trends and get insight into your psyche.

Therapy: Enlist the aid of a counselor or therapist who can help you examine your feelings and mental processes.

Setting Goals: Choosing Your Course

A potent method for personal development is to set goals that are both specific and attainable. Setting goals gives you a sense of direction, purpose, and accomplishment. Setting goals effectively entails:

Specificity: Clearly state your objectives and make sure they are measurable and concrete.

Realistic Expectations: Make ambitious but reachable goals.

Timelines: Create deadlines to keep track of your development and stay motivated.

Continual Education: Increasing Your Knowledge

Developing oneself usually entails seeking out new information and abilities. Different forms of lifelong learning exist:

Formal Education: Take into account taking classes or going after a degree in a field that interests you.

Conduct independent study by reading books, journals, and research papers on topics that interest you.

Skill Development: Make a list of the skills you wish to develop or improve, then put them into practice.

Fostering Your Well-Being Through Self-Care

The key to personal development is taking good care of your body and mind. Among the self-care techniques are:

Physical Health: Eat a balanced diet, exercise frequently, and give sleep top priority.

Mental health: Engage in stress-reduction practices like deep breathing exercises or meditation.

Emotional Well-Being: To address emotional scars and create coping mechanisms, seek therapy or counseling.

Building inner strength to be resilient

The capacity to recover from hardship and setbacks is called resilience. Resilience-building activities include:

Positivity: Strive to think positively and confront unfavorable mental patterns.

Adaptive Coping: Develop healthy coping mechanisms for stress and hardship.

Social Support: Create a large support system of friends and family.

Understanding through Reflection and Introspection

You can increase your self-awareness and foster personal development by reflecting on your experiences and conducting introspective exercises. Strategies consist of:

Regular Self-Reflection: Schedule time each day for reflection, whether it takes the form of journaling, meditation, or solitary reflection.

Seeking views: To get outside opinions on your development, ask trusted friends or mentors for their views.

Understanding and practicing self-compassion

For personal development, it's important to practice forgiveness and acceptance of your faults and past transgressions. Strategies consist of:

Self-Compassion: Recognize your humanness and imperfection and treat yourself with warmth and understanding.

Forgiveness: Set aside any pent-up animosity or hostility toward others and extend forgiveness to yourself for past transgressions.

Healthy Limits: Guarding Your Development

Protecting your personal growth requires setting and upholding healthy limits. Strategies consist of:

Communication: Be assertive yet respectful when expressing your boundaries to others.

Consistency: To stop others from straying over your limits, enforce them consistently.

A lifetime path of self-improvement and self-discovery is personal growth. It entails developing self-awareness, creating worthwhile objectives, lifelong learning, self-care, resilience, introspection, self-compassion, and the creation of sound boundaries. These methods enable people to develop their potential and set off on a transforming journey in the direction of a more contented and meaningful life. The road to personal development is a testament to each person's resiliency and capacity for improvement.

Resources for therapy and self-help

Two essential resources stand out in the pursuit of healing, personal development, and self-improvement: therapy and self-help materials. These two options provide direction, assistance, and resources for anyone looking to overcome obstacles, mend emotional wounds, and build stronger relationships.

Therapy: The Star That Points to Recovery

In therapy, commonly referred to as counseling or psychotherapy, patients interact with a licensed therapist to examine their thoughts, feelings, actions, and prior experiences in a regulated and private setting. Therapy provides a number of crucial components for recovery and personal development:

1. Expert Advice: Therapists are educated experts with knowledge of how to handle a variety of emotional and

psychological problems. They offer direction and assistance based on the particular requirements of each person.

2. Therapy provides a safe and accepting environment where people can freely express their thoughts and feelings without worrying about being judged or rejected.

3. Through therapy interactions and practices, people are able to gain insight into their mental processes, feelings, and past experiences. This promotes self-awareness.

4. Counselors provide advice on how to successfully deal with stress, anxiety, depression, and other emotional difficulties.

5. Emotional Healing: Therapy gives people a place to talk about their emotional wounds, previous trauma, and unresolved difficulties, which encourages emotional healing and progress.

6. Connection of Support: The therapeutic connection itself serves as a source of encouragement and approval, making people feel heard and understood.

Self-Help Materials: Promoting Personal Development

Self-help resources cover a wide range of books, techniques, and practices that people can use on their own to promote personal development and healing. These sources consist of:

1.Books: Self-help books span a wide range of subjects, including self-empowerment, relationship enhancement, and emotional healing. They offer information, direction, and useful exercises.

2. Workbooks: Workbooks include systematic exercises and activities that people can finish to increase self-awareness, foster coping mechanisms, and overcome certain obstacles.

3. Online Workshops and Courses: The internet offers a gold mine of workshops, webinars, and online courses

on a range of self-improvement subjects. These resources are frequently available and adaptable.

4. Support Groups: Support groups offer a sense of community and shared experiences, whether they are physical or online. They enable people to connect with others dealing with comparable difficulties and exchange knowledge and coping mechanisms.

5. Apps and Tools: A wide range of digital tools and apps are available that support mental health, mindfulness, and self-improvement. These can include journaling apps, mood-tracking devices, and meditation apps.

Allied Partners in the Journey

Self-help materials and therapy are not mutually exclusive; rather, they can support one another on the path to recovery and personal development.

Self-Help and Therapy: Many people take part in both therapy and self-help activities to support their therapeutic efforts. As an illustration, a therapist can suggest particular books or exercises as part of the recovery process.

Customized Approach: Individual preferences, requirements, and resources can be taken into account when deciding between treatment and self-help options. While some people might like the structure and direction of therapy, others could discover that self-help tools are more convenient or more suited to their schedules.

The paths to healing, personal development, and self-improvement are paved with the help of therapy and self-help materials. Therapy provides knowledgeable direction, emotional support, and a secure environment for introspection and healing. On the other side, self-help materials give people knowledge, useful tools, and a sense of agency over their own development.

Each person's route to emotional health and personal development is distinct, and the mix of therapy and self-help materials offers a flexible toolkit for pursuing it. The fact that people may use these tools to develop their potential and live healthier, more meaningful lives is proof of the human spirit's tenacity and capacity for good change.

Meditation and Mindfulness

Meditation and mindfulness techniques provide a haven of silence and self-awareness in our fast-paced and frequently chaotic world. These contemplative activities give people the skills they need to deal with life's challenges, control stress, and promote emotional wellbeing.

Being mindful means being aware of the moment

The goal of the mental exercise known as mindfulness is to develop present-moment awareness without passing judgment. It entails being aware of your ideas, feelings, physical sensations, and surroundings. The major facets of mindfulness are as follows:

1. Non-judgment: Mindfulness promotes noticing thoughts and emotions without assigning them a positive or negative connotation. This attitude of non-judgment encourages self-acceptance.

2. Acceptance: This requires recognizing that the present moment may be uncomfortable or difficult and accepting it as it is.

3. Breath Awareness: Paying attention to your breathing is a frequent mindfulness exercise that centers you in the present.

4. Self-Compassion: Self-compassion techniques, or treating oneself with care and understanding, are frequently a part of mindfulness.

A Path to Inner Calm through Meditation

A focused mental exercise called meditation can help you achieve inner peace, tranquility, and clarity. There are many different meditation techniques; however, they all have the following things in common:

1. Focused Attention: In order to maintain focus during meditation, practitioners frequently pay close attention to a particular object, mantra, or breath.

2. Observation is encouraged during meditation to enable ideas and emotions to come and go without attachment or reaction.

3. Rest: Meditation techniques frequently encourage rest, lowering stress and tension in the body and mind.

4. Self-Exploration: Meditating can be a self-discovery journey that offers understanding of one's mental processes and emotional reactions.

The advantages of meditation and mindfulness

Numerous advantages of mindfulness and meditation that support emotional health and personal development include:

1. Reduced Physiological Reaction to Stressors: Mindfulness and meditation are effective techniques for

controlling stress, encouraging relaxation, and lowering the physiological reaction to stressors.

2. Emotional Regulation: By assisting people in better understanding and controlling their emotions, they can lessen reactivity and increase emotional resilience.

3. Focus: Mindfulness and meditation improve focus and cognitive clarity, which facilitates improved judgment and problem-solving.

4. Improved Self-Awareness: By witnessing thoughts and feelings without passing judgment, people learn more about their inner lives, which promotes self-awareness.

5. Self-Compassion: Self-compassion is a mindfulness practice that encourages a kinder and more accepting connection with oneself.

6. Improved Relationships: Mindfulness and meditation can promote self-awareness and emotional control, which can lead to relationships that are stronger and more compassionate.

Including meditation and mindfulness

It can be easy and convenient to incorporate mindfulness and meditation into one's daily life.

Begin Small: Start out with brief, everyday sessions. Benefits can be obtained from even brief practice sessions.

Consistency: This is important. Whether it's in the morning, during a lunch break, or just before night, establish a pattern that works for you.

Guided Resources: There are many guided resources for mindfulness and meditation, including apps, videos, and books, which can offer direction and encouragement.

The practices of meditation and mindfulness are effective tools for guiding people on an internal journey that promotes self-awareness, emotional health, and personal development. These routines provide a haven of calm in our frequently frantic lives, enabling us to face difficulties with more resiliency and inner tranquility.

The practice of mindfulness and meditation is a testament to how the human spirit can be used to find oneself, heal, and foster stronger relationships—all of which pave the way for a life that is more meaningful and satisfying.

Divorcing Oneself from Narcotic Patterns

A significant and transforming journey, breaking free from narcissistic habits allows people to rediscover their authenticity and mend the wounds caused by narcissistic influences in their lives.

Recognizing narcissistic behaviors

Understanding what narcissistic patterns are is crucial before starting the quest to remove oneself from them. Narcissistic behaviors frequently include

1. Selfishness: Narcissistic people frequently put their own needs, wants, and self-image above all else, sometimes at the expense of other people.

2. Lack of Empathy: Narcissistic tendencies might be weak in empathy, the capacity to comprehend and share the feelings of others, which makes it difficult to emotionally connect with people.

3. Manipulation: To exert control and influence over those around them, narcissistic people sometimes use manipulation techniques like guilt-tripping or gaslighting.

4. Grandiose and inflated self-images are frequent characteristics of narcissistic behaviors, hiding underlying vulnerabilities.

5.Difficulty Accepting Criticism: Narcissistic people often respond defensively to criticism and may find it difficult to own their own shortcomings or errors.

The process of freeing oneself

It takes strength and transformation to break out of narcissistic patterns, which can be accomplished by following a few crucial steps:

1. Self-awareness: The first stage is to become aware of any narcissistic patterns that may be present in one's conduct or interpersonal interactions. This necessitates reflection and introspection.

2. Acceptance: It can be difficult, but it's essential for growth to accept that one has certain tendencies within oneself. It entails having compassion for oneself and realizing that there is always room for growth.

3. Seeking Support: Consulting a therapist, counselor, or support group can offer direction and a secure environment for examining and dealing with narcissistic patterns.

4. Setting Boundaries: It's crucial to learn how to set and preserve appropriate boundaries. This entails appreciating others' autonomy and knowing when one's responsibility ends.

5. Empathy Development: Breaking free from narcissistic behaviors requires developing empathy. This entails

actively attempting to comprehend the thoughts and viewpoints of others.

6. Regular self-reflection enables people to keep an eye on their actions, ideas, and emotional reactions and make necessary modifications.

The Influence of Authenticity and Healing

In addition to being a process of self-improvement, breaking out of narcissistic habits is also a journey toward healing and authenticity.

1. Emotional Healing: People frequently go through emotional healing as they let go of narcissistic patterns. Processing old wounds and letting go of defensive tendencies may be necessary for this.

2. Authenticity: Freedom from the restrictions of narcissistic behaviors allows people to reconnect with their true selves. Relationships become deeper and more satisfying as a result of this sincerity.

3. Freedom from narcissistic tendencies gives people the ability to take charge of their actions and decisions, paving the way for personal development and transformation.

4. Relationships that are healthier and more empathic, marked by respect for one another and an emotional connection, result from the effort to break free from narcissistic behaviors.

The Path of Liberation

It takes a significant journey of self-discovery, healing, and authenticity to release oneself from narcissistic patterns. It entails developing empathy, self-awareness, acceptance, asking for help, setting limits, and regular self-reflection. This journey enables people to let go of narcissistic habits and accept their true selves, which ultimately results in more fulfilling and lasting relationships.

The process of freeing oneself from narcissistic habits is evidence of the human spirit's capacity for development, change, and the quest for stronger, more genuine relationships with others. It is a path to freedom and empowerment that holds out the prospect of a happier and more sincere emotional future.

Adapting mental patterns

The landscape of thoughts, beliefs, and perceptions in the human mind is intricate and constantly changing. Our experiences, behaviors, and emotions are shaped by these thinking patterns, which have an impact on every part of our existence. The process of altering thought patterns stands out as a crucial activity in the context of human development and self-improvement.

The Effect of Mental Patterns

We interpret our experiences and view the world through the lenses of our thought patterns. They can be empowering or restricting, beneficial or harmful. Various thought patterns include:

1. Core Beliefs: These are ingrained opinions about the universe, other people, and ourselves. They frequently develop during childhood and have a significant impact on how we feel about ourselves.

2. Automatic Thoughts: These are the fast, unconscious ideas that pop into your head in response to different circumstances. They profoundly affect our emotions and might be either pleasant or bad.

3. Cognitive distortions are illogical and incorrect methods of thinking that frequently result in unfavorable feelings. Black-and-white thinking, catastrophizing, and mind-reading are a few examples.

4. Self-Talk: Our internal speech, or self-talk, has a significant impact on how we perceive ourselves and how we feel emotionally.

Changing thought patterns has power

Changing one's cognitive processes can have a significant impact on one's personal development and wellbeing.

1. Emotional Control: Modifying unfavorable thought patterns might result in enhanced emotional control. People can lessen anxiety, despair, and stress by confronting unreasonable ideas and automatic negative thinking.

2. Enhanced Self-Esteem: Core beliefs that diminish one's own value can be revised to increase one's own self-esteem and self-acceptance.

3. Changes in cognitive patterns give people more control over their responses and behaviors. This gives them the ability to make better decisions and set boundaries in interpersonal interactions.

4. Better Relationships: People who alter their cognitive patterns frequently interact with others with greater

empathy, compassion, and understanding, which fosters the development of stronger bonds between people.

How to Alter Your Thought Patterns?

A deliberate method for altering cognitive habits includes:

1. Making yourself aware of your thought patterns is the first step. Self-reflection and mindfulness are useful skills for this.

2. Challenge Cognitive Distortions: Determine whether your views are supported by facts and logical reasoning by examining their sources. This will help you recognize and combat cognitive distortions.

3. Reframing: Replace unfavorable or unreasonable ideas with reasonable and uplifting ones. For instance, switch from saying, "I'm a failure," to saying, "I made a mistake, but I can learn from it."

4. Positive Affirmations: Use affirmations that boost your confidence and self-worth to cultivate positive self-talk.

5. Consider receiving counseling from a cognitive-behavioral therapist (CBT) or someone with similar training if you want to change your mental habits.

Creating sensible boundaries

Our mental, emotional, and physical areas are limited by boundaries, which are invisible lines. Setting healthy boundaries stands out as a crucial component of self-care, self-respect, and the development of respectful relationships in the complex web of human connections.

The Value of Sound Boundaries

Good boundaries are necessary for a number of reasons:

1. Setting limits is a sign of respect for oneself. It shows that you care about your mental and emotional well-being.

2. Boundaries give people the freedom to choose and act in ways that are consistent with their values and needs.

3. Emotional Well-Being: By preventing people from stepping over lines that could lead to hurt or pain, maintaining boundaries helps safeguard your emotional well-being.

4. Healthy limits are the cornerstone of partnerships that are respectful and mutually gratifying. They ensure that the needs and feelings of all parties are taken into account.

Different Boundaries

Boundaries can take many different forms

1. Your personal space and physical comfort zones are defined by your physical boundaries. They can be things like physical contact, private items, and your house.

2. Emotional boundaries entail identifying and controlling your emotions on an individual basis. It implies that you are in charge of your feelings while others are in charge of theirs.

3. Mental borders: Your thoughts and intellectual space are protected by mental borders. They entail honoring your principles, convictions, and independence of thought.

4. Time Boundaries: Managing your time and energy allocation falls under the category of time boundaries. They assist you in setting priorities for your requirements and obligations.

How to Establish Healthy Boundaries

Establishing sound limits is a conscious and empowering process.

1. Self-Awareness: Start by becoming aware of your own requirements, ideals, and constraints. Setting limits is based on self-awareness.

2. Clear Communication: Be aggressive while stating your boundaries. When communicating your demands and emotions, use "I" statements.

3. Consistency: Consistently enforce your boundaries. This makes people more aware of and respectful of your boundaries.

4. Prioritize self-care in order to uphold your limits and safeguard your wellbeing.

5. Respect Others: Establishing limits doesn't involve dominating or coercing others. It's about encouraging polite and respectful interactions.

Obstacles to Setting Boundaries

It might be difficult to establish appropriate boundaries since they may require:

1. Some people are afraid that creating limits may result in confrontation. It's crucial to keep in mind that courteous dialogue usually diffuses disputes.

2. You could experience remorse for expressing your desires. Understanding that taking care of oneself is not selfish but rather self-preservation is crucial.

3. Others' Resistance: Those who regularly step over your boundaries may be resistant to change. Maintain your composure and assertively and calmly state your boundaries.

Creating sensible boundaries

Setting appropriate limits is a crucial skill in the complex dance of human relationships because it frequently affects the caliber of our interactions and our general wellbeing. Setting boundaries is an act of self-respect and self-care since they serve as the lines that define our limits.

Knowing Appropriate Boundaries

Healthy boundaries are the limits we create for ourselves on an emotional, physical, and mental level to safeguard our wellbeing and establish our personal space. These borders perform a number of vital tasks:

1. Setting limits shows that you appreciate and cherish yourself enough to look out for your needs and feelings.

2. Boundaries help you maintain your sense of independence and individuality when in a relationship.

3. They safeguard your mental health by prohibiting people from going too far or hurting your feelings.

4. Clear Communication: Respectful and clear communication are encouraged by healthy limits in partnerships.

Different Boundaries

Boundaries appear in a variety of ways:

1. Personal space, contact, and comfort are examples of physical boundaries. They decide how physically close other people can get to you.

2. How much of your emotional world you share with others is determined by your emotional boundaries. Your emotional independence is determined by them.

3. Mental limits: Your thoughts, convictions, and intellectual space are protected by mental limits. They entail honoring your beliefs and ideals.

4. Time Limits: Setting time limits will enable you to manage your time and effort in a way that respects your requirements and priorities.

How to Establish Healthy Boundaries

Self-awareness is the first step in the process of establishing healthy limits.

1. Self-awareness: recognize your needs, principles, and boundaries. Setting successful boundaries starts with self-awareness.

2. Clarity: Clearly spell out your limitations. Make strong use of "I" statements to communicate your wants and emotions.

3. Consistency: Consistently enforce your boundaries. This makes people more aware of and respectful of your boundaries.

4. Prioritize self-care in order to uphold your limits and safeguard your wellbeing.

5. Setting boundaries is not about controlling other people; rather, it's about making sure that your needs and feelings are honored.

Obstacles to Setting Boundaries

Setting good limits might be difficult for a number of reasons:

1. Some people worry that creating limits may result in confrontation. However, courteous discussion may usually resolve disagreements.

2. Guilt: When setting boundaries, especially when refusing someone, guilt may surface. Always keep in mind that caring for oneself is not selfish; it is necessary for your wellbeing.

3. Others' Resistance: Individuals who are accustomed to pushing their boundaries may encounter resistance. Remain firm, assertively, and calmly state your boundaries.

Good Things About Healthy Boundaries

Having healthy boundaries has a lot of advantages:

1. Respectful Relationships: Setting boundaries encourages considerate and respectful behavior, which strengthens bonds between people.

2. Your mental well-being is protected, which lowers stress and emotional tiredness.

3. Gaining control and empowerment over your life and decisions gives you a sense of empowerment.

4. Setting limits is a sign of self-respect since it affirms your value as a person.

How to develop self-compassion

One of the most significant virtues one may cultivate in the maze of life's struggles and self-discovery is self-compassion. This kind and compassionate way of treating oneself offers a way to emotional healing, toughness, and inner serenity.

Knowing one's own compassion

The act of treating oneself with the same compassion and understanding that one would extend to a close friend going through a challenging time is known as self-compassion. It includes three crucial components:

1. Self-kindness entails speaking kindly and compassionately to oneself rather than harshly criticizing it. It entails being a friend to oneself, particularly when facing challenges.

2. Self-compassion acknowledges that suffering and flaws are part of the universal human experience. Instead of encouraging a sense of solitude, it promotes connectedness.

3. Self-compassion involves mindfulness, or an unflinching, non-exaggerated awareness of one's own suffering. It entails accepting suffering with an open heart.

The Power of Self-Compassion for Healing

Developing self-compassion has a number of therapeutic advantages, including:

1. Self-compassion aids people in overcoming misfortune by boosting their emotional fortitude and resilience.

2. Reduced self-criticism: It replaces harsh inner dialogue with kinder inner discourse, which lessens self-criticism.

3. Enhanced Self-Esteem: Self-compassion fosters a healthier self-concept by elevating self-esteem and self-worth.

4. Emotional Regulation: It encourages improved emotional regulation, assisting people in more effective stress, anxiety, and depression management.

5. Relationships are strengthened because self-compassion frequently results in more sympathetic and understanding interactions with others.

How to develop self-compassion

Self-compassion cultivation is a deliberate practice.

1. Develop awareness as a starting point. Observe your feelings and thoughts without passing judgment.

2. Practice being kind to yourself by talking to yourself as you would a close friend. Self-criticism should be replaced with self-encouragement.

3. Common Humanity: Keep in mind that you are not struggling alone. Every person has struggles and flaws.

4. Self-care: Give your physical and mental well-being a high priority by engaging in self-care activities.

5. Self-Compassion Exercises: Practice self-compassion by meditating on your own compassion or by composing a letter of kindness to yourself.

Challenges in Self-Compassion Development

Developing self-compassion can be difficult because of:

1. Inner Critic: The inner critic, a self-critical voice, could oppose self-compassion techniques.

2. Unfamiliarity: Some people may initially find it strange because they are not used to being kind to themselves.

3. Misconceptions: It's possible for people to believe that practicing self-compassion is self-indulgent or meek. In actuality, it's an indication of emotional fortitude.

CHAPTER 7

Creating wholesome relationships

Developing trust with your kids

Healthy relationships, especially those between parents and their children, are built on trust. For both parents and kids, it may be extremely traumatic when trust is betrayed or destroyed. However, the process of reestablishing trust presents a chance for recovery, development, and the reestablishment of solid and loving ties.

The Value of Trust in Relationships Between Parents and Children

The parent-child connection requires trust for a number of reasons.

1. Emotional Safety: Children are more able to express themselves freely and honestly when they feel trusted.

2. Communication: Open and effective communication is fostered through trust, which enables parents and children to comprehend one another's needs, feelings, and viewpoints.

3. Trust lays a solid basis for a child's emotional growth, fostering a sense of security and well-being.

4. Bonding: Mutual respect and understanding are the foundation of a strong emotional link that is strengthened by trust between parents and children.

Understanding betrayed trus

There are several ways to undermine or betray trust, including by keeping your word, being dishonest, acting inconsistently, or being careless. Trust betrayal frequently results in:

1. When trust is betrayed, children may feel wounded and angry, which can lead to withdrawal, defiance, or emotional outbursts.

2. Loss of Confidence: A parent's breach of trust may cause a child to lose faith in their dependability, honesty, or concern.

3. Fear of Vulnerability: Children who have experienced trust issues with their parents may find it difficult to be open or vulnerable with them.

4. Trust concerns between parents and children may have an impact on a child's capacity to develop healthy connections in the future.

The Process of Restoring Trust

The process of reestablishing trust with your kids calls for perseverance, dedication, and introspection.

1. Recognize the behaviors or acts that resulted in the betrayal of trust and apologize for them. Express honest regret and apologize.

2. Active listening means paying attention to your child's feelings and worries without passing judgment or getting angry. Validate their feelings and encounters.

3. Be consistent in both your words and deeds. Rebuilding a sense of predictability and dependability through consistency

4. Transparency: Be honest and upfront about your goals, choices, and deeds. Don't maintain secrets or make commitments you can't keep.

5. Empathy: Consider yourself to be your child to better comprehend their viewpoint and emotions.

6. Clearly communicating and enforcing healthy boundaries in your relationship can aid in reestablishing a sense of safety.

7. Seek Professional Help: In some circumstances, consulting a family therapist or counselor who focuses on fostering trust in parent-child relationships may be helpful.

Time and patience

It takes time and patience to rebuild trust; it is not an easy task. Your child could require some time to recover and regain his or her sense of security. You must give them the time and space to regain trust at their own pace.

The Benefits of Restoring Trust

Regaining trust with your kids can result in:

1. Stronger Bond: It strengthens your emotional bond and forges a stronger, more durable bond.

2. Emotional Healing: For both parents and kids, restoring trust is a key component of emotional healing.

3. greater conversation: It encourages honest and open conversation, which facilitates greater comprehension and dispute resolution.

4. Building trust helps kids develop the resilience they need to deal with trust challenges in future relationships.

Regular Interaction

Human connection and relationships depend on communication, and open communication is the key to developing empathy, trust, and understanding.

The Value of Honest Communication

For various reasons, including parent-child dynamics, open communication is essential in partnerships.

1. Understanding: It enables people to comprehend one another's ideas, emotions, and viewpoints, which promotes empathy and kinship

2. Open communication is a key component of conflict resolution because it enables participants to discuss problems, voice their concerns, and come up with solutions.

3. Trustworthiness is a quality that is both developed and sustained through transparency and honesty.

4. Open communication creates a comfortable environment for people to express their emotions, which lowers emotional suppression and its detrimental effects.

5. Healthy Boundaries: By ensuring that people's needs and limitations are taken into account, it helps to establish and respect healthy boundaries within partnerships.

The Fundamentals of Open Communication

Open communication is based on the following tenets:

1. Giving the speaker your entire attention, trying to understand their point of view, and not interjecting or passing judgment are all examples of active listening.

2. Honesty: Transparency and candor in the exchange of ideas, emotions, and facts are essential components of open and honest communication.

3. Respect: It's important to show respect for the other person's viewpoints, emotions, and boundaries. The use of insulting language or conduct must be avoided.

4. Empathy: Identifying with the speaker's feelings and experiences helps to promote compassion and understanding.

5. Open communication necessitates a readiness to accept criticism without getting angry or confrontational.

Methods to Encourage Open Communication

It takes conscious effort to promote open communication in relationships.

1. Establish a Safe Space: Make sure that everyone may express themselves freely in a secure and judgment-free setting

2. Active listening involves paying close attention, paraphrasing to ensure comprehension, and asking clarifying questions.

3. Empathetic Reactions: Express empathy for the speaker's sentiments and experiences by acknowledging them.

4. Non-Verbal Communication: Pay attention to non-verbal indicators like body language and facial expressions because they can reveal a lot.

5. Encourage Expression: Support and validate others' expressions of ideas and emotions, even when they don't align with your own.

6. Approach conflicts with the intention of mediating them through polite communication. Avoid personal attacks and concentrate on the problem.

7. Regular Check-Ins: Arrange regular check-ins or family gatherings to communicate updates, address problems, and improve communication.

Having open communication is difficult

There are obstacles to open communication, such as:

1. Fear of Judgment: People may worry about having their opinions or feelings criticized or condemned.

2. Communication preferences and styles: Misunderstandings can result from different communication preferences and styles

3. Emotional barriers: It might be challenging to communicate effectively when experiencing strong emotions.

4. Past Stuff: Conflicts or unsolved concerns from the past may obstruct honest communication.

Remorse and amends

Conflicts and unpleasant behavior are essentially inherent in the intricate web of human connections. The willingness to apologize and make apologies, however, is what establishes the path for healing and reconciliation.

The influence of apologies

An apology is a meaningful act of acknowledging wrongdoing, expressing regret, and accepting responsibility for one's conduct. It is more than just a series of words. Why it is so important is as follows:

1. An apology confirms the offended party's damaged sentiments by confirming that their feelings and experiences are understood.

2. Ownership: It shows a person's personal ownership and accountability for their activities, which strengthens their reliability.

3. Apologizing demonstrates empathy by acknowledging the emotional toll that one's actions have on others.

4. Apologies are frequently the first step in settling disputes and advancing toward reconciliation.

The Qualities of a Sincere Apology

Several essential components make up a sincere apology:

1. Acknowledge the particular actions or behaviors that harmed others.

2. Remorse: Demonstrate genuine regret for the suffering you caused the other person.

3. Take full responsibility for your actions without assigning blame or offering justifications.

4. Empathy: Show empathy by acknowledging and comprehending the hurt party's emotions.

5. Offers to make amends or, if feasible, to resolve the issue.

Making significant changes

Actions performed to undo the damage a person's actions have done are known as amends. Why they are crucial is as follows:

1. Restitution: Making amends demonstrates a desire to put things right and address the effects of one's conduct.

2. Rebuilding Trust: Making amends is a practical way to do so and to show sincere regret.

3. Learning and Growth: It represents a dedication to developing yourself and learning from past errors.

4. Meaningful reparations can help both parties heal emotionally.

Techniques for Apologizing and Making Amends

1. Take a moment to consider your actions and their effects before apologizing.

2. Pick the Right Moment: Decide on the best moment and location to offer your apologies.

3. Be sincere: Make sure that your apology is heartfelt and sincere. Avoid making phony or forced excuses.

4. After apologizing, pay close attention to what the other person says and be receptive to their feelings and worries.

5. Take Action: If at all possible, carry out substantive reparations to redress the harm caused.

6. Learn from the experience and continue to develop yourself in order to avoid making the same mistakes again.

Problems with Apologies and Amendments

Making amends and offering an apology might be difficult because of:

1. Ego and pride: Ego and pride may make it harder to accept responsibility and offer an apology.

2. Fear of Rejection: Being afraid of being disapproved of or rejected can be daunting.

3. Situations that are Complex: In some circumstances, making reparations may be challenging or impossible, necessitating innovative alternatives.

Advocation for Good Family Dynamics

Our closest relationships are forged in the context of the family, where we also foster love, support, and progress. However, family dynamics can be complicated and fraught with difficulties.

The value of healthy family dynamics

Family harmony is important for a number of reasons, including:

1. Emotional Well-Being: A sense of security and belonging is fostered by healthy family relations, which contribute to the emotional well-being of all family members.

2. They encourage honest and effective communication to allow family members to communicate their needs, feelings, and thoughts.

3. Conflict Resolution: A framework for amicably resolving conflicts and drawing lessons from them is provided by positive family dynamics.

4. Support: During the ups and downs of life, families with healthy dynamics are a person's most reliable source of assistance

Methods for Promoting Good Family Dynamics

1. Encourage honest and direct communication among family members. Make a space where everyone in the family can feel heard and appreciated.

2. Family members should engage in active listening, which involves paying close attention to one another while refraining from interjecting or passing judgment.

3. Encourage family members to comprehend each other's thoughts and opinions to promote empathy among them.

4. Spend precious time engaging in family activities and strengthening your bonds. These experiences foster relationships and generate enduring memories.

5. Teach and practice effective conflict resolution techniques, placing special emphasis on communication, empathy, and compromise.

6. Setting Boundaries: Assist family members in establishing and upholding healthy boundaries while making sure that each person's needs and constraints are taken into account.

7. Quality Relationships: Promote wholesome interactions between family members. Teach children the importance of treating others with respect, encouragement, and gratitude.

8. Promote cultural sensitivity and respect for one another's traditions and backgrounds if your family is multicultural.

9. Honor Successes: Honor the accomplishments of every family member, no matter how great or small. Self-esteem and motivation are fostered through positive reinforcement.

10. Regular Family Meetings: Hold regular family gatherings to talk about issues, share information, and make decisions together.

Fostering Positive Family Dynamics: Challenges

Positive family dynamics may encounter a number of difficulties, such as:

1. Differences between generations can cause misunderstandings because they may hold different values, views, and communication methods.

2. External Stressors: Stressors from the outside, such as those related to employment, money, or health, can harm family ties.

3. Family members' various personalities might occasionally conflict, necessitating tolerance and understanding.

4. Unresolved concerns from the past may continue to affect family interactions now.

Promoting Personality

It is crucial to acknowledge and cherish each family member's uniqueness within the complex web of family dynamics. In addition to being a potent tool for self-expression, supporting individuality can help create families that are happier and healthier.

The Value of Supporting Individuality

It is crucial to promote individuality within the family for a number of reasons.

1. Self-Esteem: By valuing and encouraging each family member's distinctive qualities and interests, self-esteem and sense of worth are increased.

2. Self-discovery: Supporting individuality fosters self-discovery by fostering an environment where family members can explore their passions, talents, and shortcomings.

3. Respect: Encouraging individuality strengthens respect for each member of the family as a special and valued person.

4. It promotes honest and open communication since family members feel comfortable sharing their opinions and feelings.

5. Family members can approach problems with a sense of mutual respect and understanding when they embrace individuality.

Techniques for Promoting Individuality

1. Recognize Individuality: Honor the special characteristics, skills, and passions of each member of the family. Describe what makes them unique.

2. Promote open communication within the family so that everyone feels comfortable discussing their ideas, emotions, and aspirations.

3. Support Interests: Encourage and cultivate unique interests and pastimes. Give family members the chance to pursue their passions.

4. Stress the importance of respecting diversity and uniqueness within the family. instill acceptance and tolerance.

5. Set Reasonable Expectations: Don't place unreasonable demands on your family. Let them establish their own objectives and standards.

6. Encourage family members to participate in decision-making processes. Give them the freedom to decide according to their principles and interests.

7. Spend meaningful time with each family member one-on-one to better understand their individual personalities.

8. Encouragement and positive reinforcement should be given to each family member for their accomplishments and efforts.

Issues with Promoting Individuality

Challenges to promoting individualism within the family include:

1. Family standards: Prevalent family expectations or standards may stifle uniqueness.

2. Peer Pressure: Outside factors like peer pressure may stifle uniqueness.

3. Generational Differences: Individuals from different generations within a family may view individuality and self-expression differently.

4. Poor communication might prevent people from expressing their individuality and needs.

Setting a good example

Parents and other family caregivers have a significant role as role models for their children in the complex web of family dynamics. They frequently model the attitudes and behaviors that the younger generation displays. Therefore, setting an example of healthy behavior not only contributes to one's own wellbeing but also lays the groundwork for raising families that are healthier and more peaceful.

The Influence of Healthy Behavior Modeling

For a number of reasons, modeling healthy behavior within the family is quite important.

1. Parents and other adult caregivers act as the children's main role models, affecting their attitudes, values, and behaviors.

2. Communication: As children learn to express themselves in a positive way, healthy behavior models encourage honest and effective family communication.

3. Resolution of Conflicts: Parents and other primary caregivers typically model effective conflict resolution techniques for children.

4. Emotional Well-Being: Promoting appropriate emotional expression and coping skills by example benefits the emotional health of the entire family.

5. Self-Esteem: By studying caregivers who practice self-care and self-compassion, one can develop a positive self-image and self-esteem.

Methods for Demonstrating Healthy Behavior

1. Give self-care and self-compassion a priority. Showcase the value of looking after one's physical and emotional health.

2. Healthy Communication: Set a good example for your family by engaging in respectful conversation while actively listening and showing empathy.

3. Demonstrate effective dispute resolution techniques, placing special emphasis on compromise, negotiation, and problem-solving.

4. Encourage unrestricted emotional expression by letting family members express their emotions without fear of criticism.

5. discussing and demonstrating ethical behavior that is consistent with the family's values and guiding principles.

6. Positivity in Relationships: Demonstrate a positive and polite attitude toward others, especially partners, friends, and members of your extended family.

7. Lifelong Learning: Promote lifelong learning and personal development by highlighting the importance of curiosity and the development of oneself.

8. Responsibility: Be accountable for your choices and actions by taking ownership of them.

Modeling Healthy Behavior: Challenges

Family modeling of good conduct can provide a number of difficulties, such as:

1. External effects: Healthy behaviors modeled inside the family may be in conflict with external influences such as the media, peers, or societal conventions.

2. Parental Stress: Parents who are under a lot of stress may occasionally fail to provide a good example for their children.

3. Differences across generations in values and actions may have an impact on how family members perceive healthy behavior.

4. Communication barriers: Ineffective family communication might make it difficult to effectively model good behavior.

Fostering stronger, more peaceful families starts with setting an example of good behavior. It is an effective way to mold everyone's values, attitudes, and general wellbeing. Parents and caregivers can cultivate an atmosphere that promotes individual development, self-esteem, and resiliency within their family by placing a high priority on self-care, healthy communication, conflict resolution, emotional expression, and ethical ideals. In the end, the process of demonstrating healthy conduct provides proof of the transforming influence of positive role models in forming the relationships and lives of future generations.

Made in the USA
Las Vegas, NV
16 October 2023